Animal Young

Reptiles

Revised and updated

Rod Theodorou

Heinemann
LIBRARY

H **www.heinemann.co.uk/library**
Visit our website to find out more information about Heinemann Library books.

To order:
☎ Phone 44 (0) 1865 888066
Send a fax to 44 (0) 1865 314091
Visit the Heinemann Bookshop at www.heinemann.co.uk/library to browse our
catalogue and order online.

First published in Great Britain by Heinemann Library,
Halley Court, Jordan Hill, Oxford OX2 8EJ, part
of Harcourt Education. Heinemann is a registered
trademark of Harcourt Education Ltd.

Editorial: Clare Lewis
Design: Joanna Hinton-Malivoire
Illustration: Barry Atkinson Illustration
Picture research: Ruth Blair
Production: Sevy Ribierre

Printed and bound in China by South
China Printing Co. Ltd.

10-digit ISBN 0 431 93237 9
13-digit ISBN 978 0 431 93237 8
11 10 09 08 07
10 9 8 7 6 5 4 3 2 1

British Library Cataloguing in Publication Data
Theodorou, Rod
Animal Young: Reptiles – 2nd edition
597.9'139
A full catalogue record for this book is available from
the British Library.

Acknowledgements
The publishers would like to thank the following for
permission to reproduce photographs:
BBC: Michael Pitts p. **6**, Martha Holmes p. **7**, Tony
Pooley p. **14**, Mike Wilkes p. **23**; Bruce Coleman: Jane
Burton p. **18**; Creatas p. **4** bottom left; Digital Stock p.
4 top right and middle left; Digital Vision p. **4** bottom
right; Digital Vision p. **30**; Frank Lane: T Davidson p. **8**, J
Louwman p. **16**; Getty Images p. **4** top left and middle
right; NHPA: Daniel Heuclin p. **17**, Karl Switak p. **12**,
B Jones & M Shimlock p. **22**, Rich Kirchner p. **21**, Eric
Soder p. **24**; OSF: Michael & Patricia Fogden p. **5**, Mark
Jones p. **9**, Maurice Tibbles p. **11**, Martin Chillmaid p.
15, Z Leszczynski pp. **19**, **25**, M Deeble & V Stone p.
20; Tony Stone: Stephen Cooper p. **13**, Photolibrary.
com: James H Robinson p. **10**.

Cover photograph of a hatching Nile crocodile
reproduced with permission of Getty Images/Anup
Shah.

Every effort has been made to contact copyright holders
of any material reproduced in this book. Any omissions
will be rectified in subsequent printings if notice is given
to the publishers.

Contents

Some words are shown in bold, **like this**. You can find
out what they mean by looking in the Glossary.

Introduction

There are many different types of animals. All animals have babies. They look after their babies in different ways.

These are the six main animal groups.

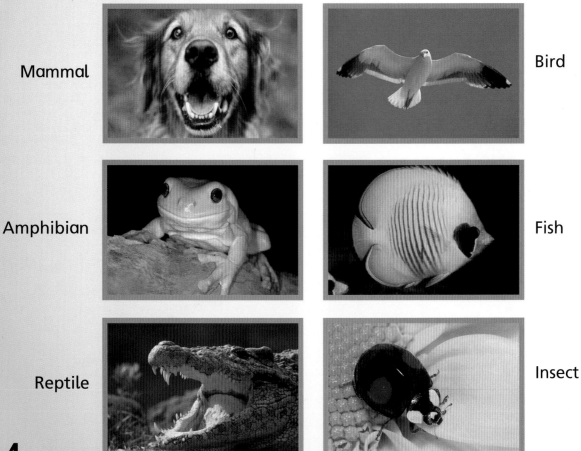

Mammal

Bird

Amphibian

Fish

Reptile

Insect

This Australian bearded lizard lives in the desert.

This book is about reptiles. Lizards, snakes, crocodiles, alligators, tortoises, and turtles are all reptiles. Most reptiles live in hot places such as deserts or rainforests.

What is a reptile?

All reptiles:

- breathe air
- are covered in **scaly** skin.

scaly skin

Komodo dragon

This marine iguana sunbathes for most of the day.

Most reptiles:

• lay eggs on land that **hatch** into babies

• are brightly coloured

• live in hot places and sunbathe to keep warm.

Building a nest

Alligators dig a hole in the middle of their nests to lay their eggs in.

Most reptiles lay their eggs in a hole in the ground or under a rock. Alligators make a huge nest out of mud and leaves.

Turtles live in the sea, but they lay their eggs on land. During the night they crawl up a beach and dig a deep hole in the sand. They lay their eggs in the hole.

flipper

This turtle uses its **flippers** to dig a hole.

Laying eggs

Most reptile eggs are white and soft like paper or **leather**. They are full of **yolk**, just like a bird's egg.

This lizard is waiting for her eggs to hatch.

Many reptile babies are eaten by **predators**, so mother reptiles lay lots and lots of eggs. This way some of their babies will escape being eaten.

This green turtle mother can lay up to 200 eggs in one night!

Looking after the eggs

Most reptiles lay their eggs and then leave them. They do not look after them or protect the **hatchlings**. A few reptiles do stay with their eggs.

This python stays with its eggs. It has wrapped itself around them to keep them warm.

Alligators attack any **predators** who want to steal their eggs.

Alligators take good care of their nests and eggs. The mother stands by the nest. She will not eat for weeks just so she can stay with her eggs.

Hatching eggs

When some baby alligators or crocodiles are ready to **hatch** they start to make grunting sounds inside the egg. The mother hears them and scratches open the nest to help them escape.

This crocodile mother is carefully cracking open her egg with her jaws.

After hatching, these baby corn snakes may rest in their broken eggs for hours before they slide away.

Baby snakes and crocodiles have a special sharp bump called an egg tooth on their **snouts**. This helps them cut or crack open their egg.

Live birth

Some reptiles do not lay eggs. Their babies grow inside them and then are born alive.

Some types of chameleon lay eggs, others give birth to live young.

When the young are born the mother does not usually look after them. The babies leave their mother and look for food.

This boa constrictor does not lay eggs. Its young are born alive.

baby snake

Finding Food

Reptile parents do not feed their **hatchlings**. As soon as young reptiles are born they have to catch their own food. They eat insects and other small animals.

This young crocodile has caught a fish.

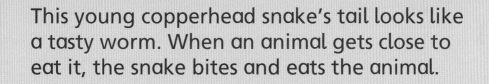

snake's tail

This young copperhead snake's tail looks like a tasty worm. When an animal gets close to eat it, the snake bites and eats the animal.

Reptile young are born strong and fast. They can hunt for food just like their parents.

Looking after the young

Crocodiles and alligators take good care of their young. The young stay together in groups. The adults watch out for **predators**, such as snakes or birds.

Sometimes Nile crocodile mothers carry their babies on their back to keep them safe.

Mother alligators look after their young for up to three years.

Alligator young call out to their parents when they need help. If a baby gets lost it makes a loud call. The large females quickly rush to find it.

Growing up

When baby turtles **hatch** they make their way to the sea. In the sea they find food and grow into adults.

Only a few turtles **survive** to grow into adults.

new skin

old skin

This grass snake has shed its skin.

As young reptiles grow they get too big for their skin. They rub against a stone. Their skin splits and comes off. New skin has grown underneath. This is called **shedding**.

Staying safe

Young lizards can drop their tails if an **enemy** attacks. If a hunter grabs them by the tail, the tail drops off and they escape. A new tail will slowly grow back.

This common wall lizard has dropped its tail.

Many other animals hunt and eat young reptiles. They stay safe by hiding or running away. If they can stay safe they will grow up and have babies of their own.

This baby chameleon is very small. It must learn how to escape **predators**.

Reptile life cycles

This is how a crocodile grows up.
The baby hatches from an egg.

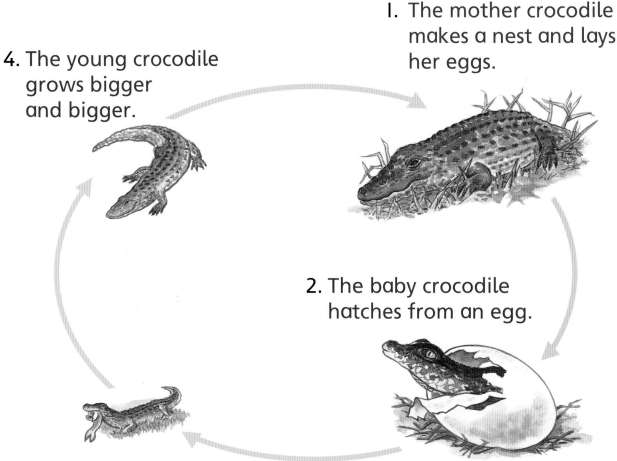

4. The young crocodile grows bigger and bigger.

1. The mother crocodile makes a nest and lays her eggs.

2. The baby crocodile hatches from an egg.

3. The baby crocodile can hunt its own food.

This is how a boa constrictor grows up.
The baby is born alive.

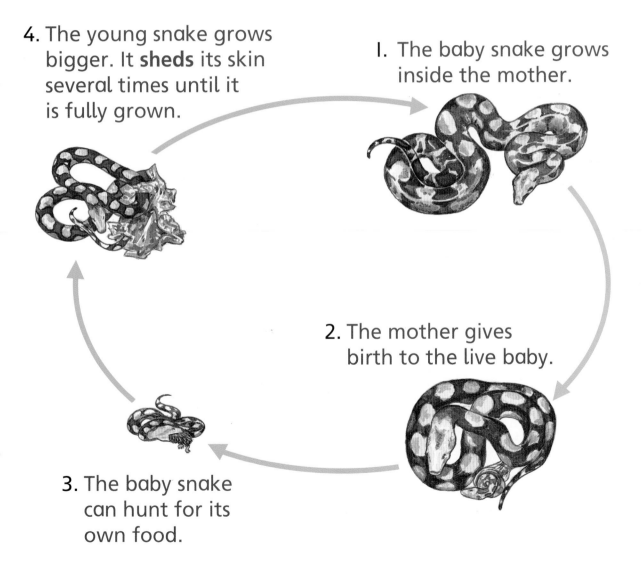

4. The young snake grows bigger. It **sheds** its skin several times until it is fully grown.

1. The baby snake grows inside the mother.

2. The mother gives birth to the live baby.

3. The baby snake can hunt for its own food.

Reptiles and other animals

		REPTILES	
WHAT THEY LOOK LIKE:	Bones inside body	all	
	Number of legs	4 or none	
	Hair on body	none	
	Scaly skin	all	
	Wings	none	
	Feathers	none	
WHERE THEY LIVE:	On land	most	
	In water	some	
HOW THEY ARE BORN:	Grows babies inside body	some	
	Lays eggs	most	
HOW THEY FEED YOUNG:	Feeds baby milk	none	
	Brings baby food	none	

MAMMALS	INSECTS	AMPHIBIANS	BIRDS	FISH
all	none	all	all	all
none, 2, or 4	6	4 or none	2	none
all	all	none	none	none
none	none	none	none	most
some	most	none	all	none
none	none	none	all	none
most	most	most	all	none
some	some	some	none	all
most	some	few	none	some
few	most	most	all	most
all	none	none	none	none
most	some	none	most	none

Remarkable reptiles!

- Reptiles do not need to eat very much. Some snakes only eat once every few months.

- Some lizards can squirt blood out of their eyes to scare away enemies.

- The giant tortoise can live for over 150 years.

Giant tortoise

Glossary

enemy an animal that will kill another animal for food or for its home

flipper the flat parts of a reptile's body that stick out and are used for swimming

hatch to be born from an egg

hatchling name for a baby when it has just been born from an egg

leather tough and hard animal skin that is used to make shoes, clothes and bags

predator an animal that hunts and kills other animals for food

scaly skin that is covered with small, flat pieces of hard, dry skin

shed to lose an old layer of skin when a new, bigger one has grown

snout a long nose

survive to stay alive

yolk part of an egg that is food for a baby animal

Find out more

Books

Life Cycles: The Life of a Sea Turtle, Claire Hibbert (Raintree, 2005)

Under My Feet: Snakes, Patricia Whitehouse (Raintree, 2003)

Wild World: Watching Cobras in Asia, Louise and Richard Spilsbury (Heinemann Library, 2006)

Website

nationalzoo.si.edu/Animals/ReptilesAmphibians/ForKids

Index